T0197648

My Animal ABC Book

Daniel Guzman Escobar

AuthorHouse™
1663 Liberty Drive
Bloomington, IN 47403
www.authorhouse.com
Phone: 833-262-8899

Because of the dynamic nature of the Internet, any web addresses or links contained in this book may have changed since publication and may no longer be valid. The views expressed in this work are solely those of the author and do not necessarily reflect the views of the publisher, and the publisher hereby disclaims any responsibility for them.

Any people depicted in stock imagery provided by Getty Images are models, and such images are being used for illustrative purposes only.
Certain stock imagery © Getty Images.

This book is printed on acid-free paper.

ISBN: 978-1-6655-3172-6 (sc)
ISBN: 978-1-6655-3173-3 (e)

Library of Congress Control Number: 2021914168

Print information available on the last page.

Published by AuthorHouse 07/13/2021

authorHOUSE

This book is dedicated to my son, Isaac, who was born prematurely at 24 weeks, weighing 1lb 4 oz. The illustrations began in a sketchbook that I would draw in while visiting Isaac in the NICU during his 138-day hospital stay. What began as a simple sketch to keep by his bedside, quickly developed into a series. After having completed several, I thought that these would make a great ABC book. It was then that these Illustrations were realized with great love and care.

It is my wish that your child will enjoy this book again and again just as much as Isaac does.

Much love,

-Daniel

Aa

Armadillo

Bear

Cat

Dog

E e

Elephant

Fox

Giraffe

Hh

Hummingbird

Ii

Iguana

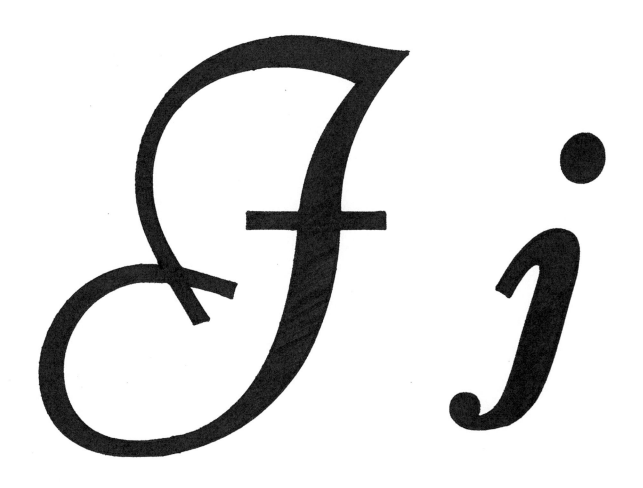

Jaguar

Kangaroo

Lion

Mm

Monkey

Newt

Owl

Peacock

Quetzal

Rabbit

Sloth

T t

Tiger

U u

Urial

Vulture

Ww

Whale

X x

X-ray Tetra

Yak

Zz

Zebra

Printed in the United States
by Baker & Taylor Publisher Services